PARABLES

OF
THE **KINGDOM**

PART ONE

Catherine Upchurch

LITTLE ROCK SCRIPTURE STUDY

*A ministry of the Diocese of Little Rock
in partnership with Liturgical Press*

DIOCESE OF LITTLE ROCK

2500 North Tyler Street • P.O. Box 7565 • Little Rock, Arkansas 72217 • (501) 664-0340 Fax (501) 664-6304

Dear Friends in Christ,

Sacred Scripture is a wealth of inspired wisdom expressing Christian truths which challenge us to deepen our relationship with God. Although the Bible can be intimidating, it is important that we study God's word in the Scriptures, because it is the basis of our faith and offers us the thoughts and experiences of Christians past and present. It is God speaking to us through the insights of Church fathers and later saints.

I am pleased to present this study guide from Little Rock Scripture Study to serve as an aid for reflection and contemplation in your reading of Scripture. At the same time, the guide will give you insight into how to apply what you have read to your life today.

I encourage you to read Sacred Scripture slowly and reflectively so that it can penetrate your heart and mind. It is my hope that the Word of God will empower you as Christians to live a life worthy of your call as a child of God and a member of the body of Christ.

Sincerely in Christ,

✢ Anthony B. Taylor
Bishop of Little Rock

Sacred Scripture

"The Church has always venerated the divine Scriptures just as she venerates the body of the Lord, since from the table of both the word of God and of the body of Christ she unceasingly receives and offers to the faithful the bread of life, especially in the sacred liturgy. She has always regarded the Scriptures together with sacred tradition as the supreme rule of faith, and will ever do so. For, inspired by God and committed once and for all to writing, they impart the word of God Himself without change, and make the voice of the Holy Spirit resound in the words of the prophets and apostles. Therefore, like the Christian religion itself, all the preaching of the Church must be nourished and ruled by sacred Scripture. For in the sacred books, the Father who is in heaven meets His children with great love and speaks with them; and the force and power in the word of God is so great that it remains the support and energy of the Church, the strength of faith for her sons, the food of the soul, the pure and perennial source of spiritual life."

Vatican II, Dogmatic Constitution on Divine Revelation, no. 21.

INTERPRETATION OF SACRED SCRIPTURE

"Since God speaks in sacred Scripture through men in human fashion, the interpreter of sacred Scripture, in order to see clearly what God wanted to communicate to us, should carefully investigate what meaning the sacred writers really intended, and what God wanted to manifest by means of their words.

"Those who search out the intention of the sacred writers must, among other things, have regard for 'literary forms.' For truth is proposed and expressed in a variety of ways, depending on whether a text is history of one kind or another, or whether its form is that of prophecy, poetry, or some other type of speech. The interpreter must investigate what meaning the sacred writer intended to express and actually expressed in particular circumstances as he used contemporary literary forms in accordance with the situation of his own time and culture. For the correct understanding of what the sacred author wanted to assert, due attention must be paid to the customary and characteristic styles of perceiving, speaking, and narrating which prevailed at the time of the sacred writer, and to the customs men normally followed in that period in their everyday dealings with one another."

Vatican II, Dogmatic Constitution on Divine Revelation, no. 12.

Instructions

MATERIALS FOR THE STUDY

This Study Guide: Parables of the Kingdom—Part One

Bible: The New American Bible with Revised New Testament or The New Jerusalem Bible is recommended. Paraphrased editions are discouraged as they offer little if any help when facing difficult textual questions. Choose a Bible you feel free to write in or underline.

Commentary: *Parables of the Kingdom* by Mary Ann Getty-Sullivan (Liturgical Press) is used with this study. The assigned pages are found at the beginning of each lesson.

ADDITIONAL MATERIALS

Bible Dictionary: *The Dictionary of the Bible* by John L. McKenzie (Simon & Schuster) is highly recommended as a reference.

Notebook: A notebook may be used for lecture notes and your personal reflections.

WEEKLY LESSONS

Lesson 1—Introduction to the Parables in Mark and Matthew
Lesson 2—Parables in the Gospel of Mark

Lesson 3—More Parables in the Gospel of Mark
Lesson 4—Parables Matthew Shared with Mark
Lesson 5—More Parables Matthew Shared with Mark

YOUR DAILY PERSONAL STUDY

The first step is prayer. Open your heart and mind to God. Reading Scripture is an opportunity to listen to God who loves you. Pray that the same Holy Spirit who guided the formation of Scripture will inspire you to correctly understand what you read and empower you to make what you read a part of your life.

The next step is commitment. Daily spiritual food is as necessary as food for the body. This study is divided into daily units. Schedule a regular time and place for your study, as free from distractions as possible. Allow about twenty minutes a day. Make it a daily appointment with God.

As you begin each lesson read the assigned chapters of Scripture found at the beginning of each lesson, the footnotes in your Bible, and then the indicated pages of the commentary. This preparation will give you an overview of the entire lesson and help you to appreciate the context of individual passages.

As you reflect on Scripture, ask yourself these four questions:

1. *What does the Scripture passage say?*
   Read the passage slowly and reflectively. Use your imagination to picture the scene or enter into it.

2. *What does the Scripture passage mean?*
   Read the footnotes and the commentary to help you understand what the sacred writers intended and what God wanted to communicate by means of their words.

3. *What does the Scripture passage mean to me?*
   Meditate on the passage. God's Word is living and powerful. What is God saying to you today? How does the Scripture passage apply to your life today?

4. *What am I going to do about it?*
   Try to discover how God may be challenging you in this passage. An encounter with God contains a challenge to know God's will and follow it more closely in daily life.

THE QUESTIONS ASSIGNED FOR EACH DAY

Read the questions and references for each day. The questions are designed to help you listen to God's Word and to prepare you for the weekly small-group discussion.

Some of the questions can be answered briefly and objectively by referring to the Bible references and the commentary *(What does the passage say?)*. Some will lead you to a better understanding of how the Scriptures apply to the Church, sacraments, and society *(What does the passage mean?)*. Some questions will invite you to consider how God's Word challenges or supports you in your relationships with God and others *(What does the passage mean to me?)*. Finally, the questions will lead you to examine your actions in light of Scripture *(What am I going to do about it?)*.

Write your responses in this study guide or in a notebook to help you clarify and organize your thoughts and feelings.

THE WEEKLY SMALL-GROUP MEETING

The weekly small-group sharing is the heart of the Little Rock Scripture Study Program. Participants gather in small groups to share the results of praying, reading, and reflecting on Scripture and on the assigned questions. The goal of the discussion is for group members to be strengthened and nourished individually and as a community through sharing how God's Word speaks to them and affects their daily lives. The daily study questions will guide the discussion; it is not necessary to discuss all the questions.

All members share the responsibility of creating an atmosphere of loving support and trust in the group by respecting the opinions and experiences of others, and by affirming and encouraging one another. The simple shared prayer that begins and ends each small group meeting also helps create the open and trusting environment in which group members can share their faith deeply and grow in the study of God's Word.

A distinctive feature of this program is its emphasis on and trust in God's presence working in and through each member. Sharing responses to God's presence in the Word and in others can bring about remarkable growth and transformation.

THE WRAP-UP LECTURE

The lecture is designed to develop and clarify the themes of each lesson. It is not intended to be the focus of the group's discussion. For this reason, the lecture always occurs *after* the small group discussion. If several small groups meet at one time, the groups may gather in a central location to listen to the lecture.

Lectures may be presented by a local speaker. They are also available in audio form on CD and in visual form on DVD.

Introduction to the Parables in Mark and Matthew

PARABLES OF THE KINGDOM, PAGES I–I5

(This first lesson relies heavily on the commentary for a basic understanding and appreciation for parables. Subsequent lessons will look more directly at biblical texts.)

Day I

1. What attracted you to this particular Bible study about parables?

2. What is your favorite parable from the ministry of Jesus? Why?

3. When have you used a story to illustrate a point? How does this experience help you to appreciate the way that Jesus used parables in his public life?

Day 2

4. In the Synoptic Gospels of Matthew, Mark, and Luke, what kinds of writing could be considered parables?

5. Parables characteristically use common experiences and draw comparisons or analogies to describe something that is not clearly known or fully understood. Jesus used images from his own time and culture. Look up the following references and indicate what you learn about being a disciple: Matt 5:13-16; 6:19-21; 12:33-37.

6. What modern images or comparisons could you use that would describe for today's listeners what it means to be a disciple? Use your imagination.

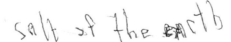

Salt of the earth

Day 3

7. Return to the parable you identified as one of your favorites when you began this study. What in that particular parable provides the twist or the surprise?

8. One of the characteristics of parables is that they have the capacity to call listeners to conversion. When has a parable of Jesus had this effect in your life? Did a homily help to bring out this aspect of the parable for you?

9. The author of the commentary states that "parables are one of Jesus' preferred tools to involve hearers in the process of revelation" (p. 5). What kind of disposition do you bring to Bible study or to liturgy that helps remind you that you are an active participant in God's revelation?

Day 4

10. What general impressions or ideas do you associate with the word "kingdom" as it is used in our world today?

11. In what general ways do modern concepts of "kingdom" differ from the biblical concept of the kingdom as in the "kingdom of God"? (See Ps 145:10-13; Mic 4:1-7; Mark 1:15; Rom 14:17.)

12. What kinds of "costs" are associated with being children of God's kingdom? (See Matt 5:20; 7:21; 18:3-5.)

Right vous & good or you wont enter into heaven

Day 5

13. What evidence is there that Jesus did not invent parables or was not the first to use them as a call to faithfulness? (See 2 Sam 12:1-7; Job; Jonah.)

14. In what New Testament books are the parables of Jesus found?

15. a) Summarize the criteria used by scholars to identify the parables that were authentically from Jesus. (See commentary, pages 11–12.)

    b) Why would other parables be included in the gospel accounts?

Day 6

16. The gospels reflect each evangelist's concerns about Christology and discipleship. How do you understand these two terms? (See commentary, page 13.)

17. Review the common themes of the parables found on page 14 of the commentary. Do you have any confusion that the group might help to clarify?

18. How does the naming of a parable sometimes focus one's expectations about its lessons? Give an example.

13.

14. Matthew, Mark & Luke
15. (A) hi-lited an page 11- commentary

    (B) indicates of things to come

16. hi-lite pg 13
17. ht=lite pg 14

18. hi-lite bottom of pg 14/15

Parables in the Gospel of Mark

MARK 4:1-20
PARABLES OF THE KINGDOM, PAGES 16–34

Day 1

1. Equipped with a better understanding of parables from the previous lesson, have your expectations for this study changed at all?

2. What do we know about the conditions surrounding the writing of the Gospel of Mark?

3. a) How does Mark portray the disciples and their understanding of Jesus and his teaching? (See Mark 6:34-52; 8:27-33; 9:31-32.)

   b) Who is the first to truly proclaim the identity of Jesus in Mark's gospel, and what is the context (Mark 15:33-39)?

Day 2

4. Mark 4:1-2 sets the stage for the first parables of Jesus in the Gospel of Mark. Look closely at the wording. How does it set the stage for the importance of Jesus' teaching?

5. Given how we think of teachers and their positions in classrooms and lecture halls, does it surprise you to learn that Jesus was seated when he taught the crowds (Mark 4:1)?

6. Have you ever found yourself in a crowd of people pressing to see some event or to hear a speaker? What kind of energy is in such a crowd? Does that tell you anything about the level of anticipation that is being depicted as Jesus begins to teach in Mark 4?

Day 3

7. What is the significance of Jesus beginning his teaching with the words "Hear this" (4:3)? (See Deut 6:4-5; also Deut 5:1; 9:1; 20:3-4.)

8. The parable of the sower in Mark 4:3-8 is filled with ideas and terms that are repeated in various ways. In your experience, when has repetition been helpful to you?

9. What is the significance of the increasing yield from the seed sown in rich soil (Mark 4:8)?

Day 4

10. How would the parable of the sower be particularly important in speaking to Mark's audience during the mid-'60s in the Roman Empire?

11. Since the meaning of the parable can seem quite obvious, what is Mark's purpose in having Jesus take the disciples aside for further explanation (Mark 4:10-13)? (See 7:17, 33; 9:27-29; 10:32.)

12. How can the parables of Jesus both include and exclude those who hear them (Mark 4:11-12)? What seems to be the key to understanding them? (See Matt 13:11.)

8. in studying for a test - repetition learned psalm 23 by repetition

9. What goes into a body its fine what come out of mouth & actions that can be hurtful.

Day 5

13. Is the "mystery of the kingdom of God" (Mark 4:11) something that can be defined? If so, what is the purpose? If not, what is this "mystery" about?

14. Summarize the various ways of understanding Jesus' use of Isaiah 6:9 (Mark 4:12). (See Mark 8:17-18; Jer 5:21.) Is it fair to assume that parables cause misunderstanding and hardness of heart, or that misunderstanding results because of hardness of heart?

15. In the explanation of the parable of the sower (Mark 4:14-20), how does an appreciation for other scriptural allusions help to unfold its meaning? (See 3:23-29; 10:17-22; 13:7-8; Gen 3:18.)

Day 6

16. What is required of those who hear God's Word (4:20)? (See 3:31; Luke 8:19-21; 11:27-28.)

17. In what ways are you preparing the soil of your life so that it can receive the Word and bear fruit?

18. After studying Mark's version of the parable of the sower, what would you want to name the parable? And how does that indicate your particular understanding or appreciation of the parable?

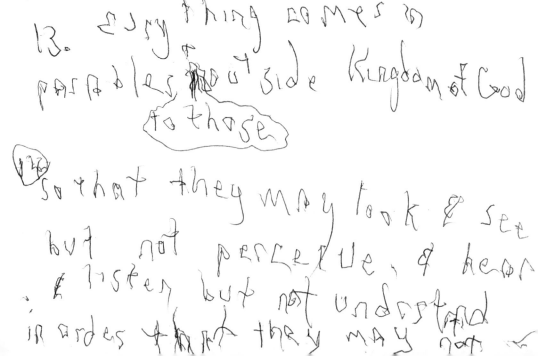

13. Everything comes in parables about side Kingdom of God to those

14. So that they may look & see but not perceive, & hear & listen but not understand in order that they may not

be converted & be forgiven

More Parables in the Gospel of Mark

MARK 4:21-34; 12:1-12; 13:28-37
PARABLES OF THE KINGDOM, PAGES 34–48

Day 1

1. Is there anything in particular from last week's discussion or wrap-up lecture that you feel will help you as you continue studying the parables?

2. What makes a lamp lighting the darkness (Mark 4:21-22) a particularly good image to use when describing the kingdom of God? (See John 8:12; Eph 5:8-9.)

3. Have you experienced the truth of Mark 4:24-25? If so, how?

Day 2

4. Identify one or two major differences in how the seed and sower are portrayed in Mark 4:26-29 as opposed to Mark 4:3-9.

5. When you consider the tiny mustard seed and the strong protective plant that it produces (Mark 4:30-32), what impressions are you given about the kingdom of God? (See Matt 13:31-32.)

6. Based on your own observation of growth in the natural world, why do you suppose Jesus employed these very common images?

Day 3

7. Each time that the owner of the vineyard sends a messenger to the tenant farmers, the reader's expectations are intensified (Mark 12:2-8). Why is the technique of escalating repetition effective? (See other examples in Gen 18:20-32; Matt 4:1-11.)

8. Jesus used rhetorical questions to involve his audience (Mark 12:9, 10, 15). When have you been drawn to ponder a new idea or insight because a speaker or writer asked good questions?

9. a) Why would scholars believe that the original setting of the parable of the tenants (Mark 12:1-12) was probably Galilee?

   b) Why would Mark have moved the parable from its original setting in Galilee to the city of Jerusalem (Mark 11:27)? What do you know about the city and about its importance in the story of Jesus? (See 10:32-34; 11:15-19, 27-33; 13:1-2; 15:33-39.)

Day 4

10. Mark makes it clear in his account of the vineyard and the tenant farmers that Jesus employed an Old Testament image (see Isa 5:1-7). In what ways is the ancient story adapted for new purposes?

11. What can we learn about the prophets in Israel to help us understand the parable of the vineyard and the tenant farmers (Mark 12:1-12)? (See Amos 5:16-18; Isa 5:18-26; Jer 2:29-37; 5:14-17.)

12. Who is the object of punishment in the parable of the vineyard owner and the tenants, and who do they symbolize (Mark 12:9)?

Day 5

13. In Mark 12:10-11, Jesus quotes Psalm 118:22-23. This same psalm is frequently part of Lenten worship. Why would a passage about rejecting the cornerstone be appropriate for Lent?

14. The parables of the fig tree and the doorkeeper are part of Mark's eschatological discourse in chapter 13. What is the purpose of this discourse? (See Bible footnotes and the commentary for this course.)

15. In your opinion, which of the two parables in Mark 13:28-37 is the most effective in communicating the need for watchfulness? Why?

Day 6

16. What insights can you find about the importance of watchmen from the following passages? (See Ps 127:1; Ezek 3:17-19; 33:1-9; Heb 13:17.)

17. When has watchfulness been an important part of your spiritual growth? (See Ps 59:10-11; 130:5-6; Matt 24:42-44.)

18. Summarize what you have learned about Jesus' use of parables in the Gospel of Mark. What one or two things would you want to remember that seem important?

Parables Matthew Shared with Mark

MATT 13:1-23
PARABLES OF THE KINGDOM, PAGES 49–62

Day 1

1. Do you have any lingering questions from the previous session?

2. What are the probable sources for Matthew's gospel?

3. Why is the late first-century division between Judaism and Christianity such an important part of understanding Matthew's gospel and his understanding of Jesus?

Day 2

4. Review the themes of Matthew's gospel, outlined on pages 51–53 of your commentary. What do you already notice that distinguishes this gospel from that of Mark?

5. Why is chapter 13 considered a turning point in the Gospel of Matthew?

6. One important difference between Matthew's telling of the parable of sowings and Mark's telling is how the parable is introduced (Mark 3:4, "Hear this!" and Matt 13:1, "On that day . . ."). What is the significance of "On that day"? (See Isa 2:12; 10:20; 13:9; Amos 5:18-20.)

a. It substituted Jesus the teacher 4 Jesus the man of action.

It solved writers problem as to the apparent failure of the program of the prophets.

It united several sources into one.

4. Mark paints bleak picture of discipleship failing where Matthew presents a more positive one.

Day 3

7. Mark's version of the parable of the sowings says the seed in rich soil produced thirty, sixty, and even one hundred yield. What is the purpose of Matthew reversing the order of the yield (Matt 13:8)?

8. Think of a recent time when your efforts produced a larger or more abundant yield than you expected. How do you make sense of that? What do you learn from such abundance that can deepen your spiritual life?

9. The parable of the sower emphasizes that the Word of God is effective (Matt 13:8; Mark 4:8), even when it initially seems to fall on deaf ears (poor soil). How have you experienced the effectiveness of God's word in your own life? (See Isa 55:10-11.)

Day 4

10. The disciples of Jesus approached him with their desire for understanding (Matt 13:10). In what circumstances do you usually approach Jesus and what is your attitude? (See Matt 15:12; Heb 4:15-16; 7:25; 10:19-22.)

11. What kinds of things in modern life tend to promote a hardening of heart (Matt 13:14-15)? What prevents us from seeing and hearing the things that God is revealing? (See Ps 95:8-9; Heb 3:12-14.)

12. Have you ever had an experience where you felt you truly heard or saw things as Jesus sees them (Matt 13:16)? Please describe.

Day 5

13. What does Matthew add to Mark's version of the purpose of parables (Matt 13:16)?

14. Describe a person whom you know who demonstrates that the Word of God has produced blessings in his or her life.

15. While Mark emphasizes that discipleship is about carrying the cross (Mark 8:34-35), Matthew adds a focus on the understanding and obedient response to the teachings of Jesus (Matt 13:16, 23; 13:52; 16:15-17). How can we deepen our understanding of God's life and learn to respond more heartily? What kinds of things are you doing to respond to this call?

Be patient

Day 6

16. Imagine the arid desert landscape that dominates most of the Middle East. What sort of an appreciation do you think natives of that area would have for a parable about a rich harvest?

17. The gospels often paint a picture of a deeply religious community in Israel, but one that is lacking truly spiritual leadership. How would the parables of Jesus have been a source of hope for so many of the common people?

13. Don't take anything or you'll 4 granted or lose it

15. Always look 4 the good in people

16. Very Appreciative

17. People should Act on A Possitive understanding of his word

LESSON 5

More Parables Matthew Shared with Mark

MATT 13:24-35, 44-52; 21:33-46; 24:32-44
PARABLES OF THE KINGDOM, PAGES 62–76

Day 1

1. What nuances have you already seen in the way Matthew handles parables originally found in the Gospel of Mark?

2. As you read the parable of the weeds and the wheat (Matt 13:24-30), what is your initial response? Does it seem logical or illogical? How does your response "set up" an expectation and emphasize the "twist" to the teaching?

3. The parable of the sower (Matt 13:1-9; Mark 4:1-9) deals with how the Word produces a harvest. The parable of the weeds and wheat (Matt 13:24-30) deals with the existence of evil among good. Are these questions that you are concerned about as you live out your discipleship?

Day 2

4. What is the wisdom in allowing the weeds to grow alongside the wheat (Matt 13:30, 40-43) or collecting all the fish caught in the net only to separate them later (Matt 13:47-50)?

5. What is the danger of too quickly assuming who in our communities might be considered just (the wheat) and who might be considered evil (the weeds)?

6. How do you balance the need to identify and avoid evil with the need to refrain from judging others? (See Matt 7:1-5; Rom 12:2; 14:10-12; 1 Cor 5:11-13; Gal 6:4-5.)

32

Day 3

7. What is the significance of both Matthew and Luke pairing the parable of the mustard seed with that of the leaven (Matt 13:31-33; Luke 13:18-21)?

8. Put yourself in the position of the original hearers of the parable, hearers who would have been familiar with their own sacred writings. How would this familiarity affect their understanding of the image used by Matthew in 13:32? (See Ps 104:10-12; Ezek 17:22-24; 31:2-9; Dan 4:7-22.)

9. When there is a mention of leaven or yeast in Scripture it often serves as a reminder of the central experience of God's people leaving Egypt and not having time to add leaven to their dough (Exod 12:31-34). To arrive in a new kingdom they had no time to wait for the dough to rise. In the parable of Matthew 13:33, leaven is a sign of the kingdom. Comment on the way Jesus reverses the association many would have had.

Day 4

10. The parables of the treasure, the pearl, and the fishing net (Matt 13:44-49) all point to the value of the kingdom of God. What do you consider of great value that you might search for, leaving all else behind? Does this help you to consider whether you value God's kingdom in the same way?

11. Summarize the possible meanings of "the new and the old" that are brought from the storeroom (Matt 13:52).

12. In your journey of faith, in what ways do you value both "the new and the old"?

Day 5

13. Why do you suppose people in his own region rejected Jesus and doubted his teaching authority (Matt 13:54-58)? (See John 4:43-44; 6:41-42.) And who in our own communities might we be in danger of doubting for similar reasons?

14. In Matthew's version of the parable of the tenants, the Jewish religious leaders end up identifying themselves as the tenant farmers who have failed the vineyard (Matt 21:40-46).

    a) How do the chief priests and Pharisees react when they recognize themselves as the accused?

    b) How can we in the church today assure that we are worthy tenants of the vineyard, worthy citizens of the kingdom of God?

15. In contrast to the chief priests and Pharisees, how did another Jewish leader, King David, respond when he was trapped in his own guilt? (See 2 Sam 12:1-13.)

Day 6

16. What is the connection between Jesus' title as "Son of Man" (Matt 24:36-44) and the expectations for his return? (See Matt 16:13-17, 26-28; 19:27-28; 24:23-28; Dan 7:13-14.)

17. After studying a limited number of parables in the Gospels of Mark and Matthew, what are two or three dominant lessons you have learned about what Jesus meant by the kingdom of God or the kingdom of heaven?

18. In what ways do the parables of Jesus continue to draw in listeners and readers? Why are they still effective?

370

NOTES

ABBREVIATIONS

Books of the Bible

Gen—Genesis
Exod—Exodus
Lev—Leviticus
Num—Numbers
Deut—Deuteronomy
Josh—Joshua
Judg—Judges
Ruth—Ruth
1 Sam—1 Samuel
2 Sam—2 Samuel
1 Kgs—1 Kings
2 Kgs—2 Kings
1 Chr—1 Chronicles
2 Chr—2 Chronicles
Ezra—Ezra
Neh—Nehemiah
Tob—Tobit
Jdt—Judith
Esth—Esther
1 Macc—1 Maccabees
2 Macc—2 Maccabees
Job—Job
Ps(s)—Psalm(s)
Prov—Proverbs
Eccl—Ecclesiastes
Song—Song of Songs
Wis—Wisdom
Sir—Sirach
Isa—Isaiah
Jer—Jeremiah
Lam—Lamentations
Bar—Baruch
Ezek—Ezekiel
Dan—Daniel
Hos—Hosea
Joel—Joel
Amos—Amos

Obad—Obadiah
Jonah—Jonah
Mic—Micah
Nah—Nahum
Hab—Habakkuk
Zeph—Zephaniah
Hag—Haggai
Zech—Zechariah
Mal—Malachi
Matt—Matthew
Mark—Mark
Luke—Luke
John—John
Acts—Acts
Rom—Romans
1 Cor—1 Corinthians
2 Cor—2 Corinthians
Gal—Galatians
Eph—Ephesians
Phil—Philippians
Col—Colossians
1 Thess—1 Thessalonians
2 Thess—2 Thessalonians
1 Tim—1 Timothy
2 Tim—2 Timothy
Titus—Titus
Phlm—Philemon
Heb—Hebrews
Jas—James
1 Pet—1 Peter
2 Pet—2 Peter
1 John—1 John
2 John—2 John
3 John—3 John
Jude—Jude
Rev—Revelation